Inspirations

Kenneth Wheeler

Edited by Steve Wheeler

First published by
Wheelsong Books
4 Willow Close, Plymouth PL3 6EY, United Kingdom

First published in 2020

Print ISBN 979-86672-5836-0

—

Acknowledgements

My thanks go out to the people in my life who together made this book of reflections and poetry possible.

To my dear, late wife Ruth who encouraged me in my writing. She injected a spark of hope into what would have otherwise been a dull life.

To my son Steve who gave me an iPad on my 85th birthday and said: "Write your story Dad. There's a story in every one of us."

Most importantly, my eternal thanks go to my Lord and Saviour Jesus Christ, without whom I would have nothing. Praise and glory to His Name.

I hope you will enjoy reading these reflections and poems as much as I have enjoyed writing them.

God bless you

Kenneth R V Wheeler
Plymouth, UK
July 2020

Foreword

When I gave my Dad an iPad as a birthday gift several years back, I could never have predicted what he would do with it. An expensive chopping board? A door wedge? I'm being facetious of course. I knew Dad was already a prolific writer. He had already crafted several short stories, using a pen and reams of lined paper. These were then turned into computer files by a never ending army of unsuspecting 'types' whom he press-ganged into his literary cause.

Those poor, poor people. They never knew what hit them.

Now, armed with his iPad, my Dad could wreak all that havoc on his own without any help from anyone. What's more, he was now connected to the Internet! Oh boy. I'm afraid it was me that introduced him to Facebook and now he was connected to people everywhere across the planet! He learnt how to blog using the platform. This was something I hadn't anticipated.

Within a short time, he was blogging every day, writing about his time serving in the Royal Air Force, his years as a school boy during the Plymouth Blitz (his school was bombed and he had no place to continue his education for many months) and his very large, and not very well off family, living in close quarters with his 10 older brothers and sisters in a cramped house near the Marine barracks in Stonehouse. And he was sharing his stories with the world.

In his life, being born into a poor family, my Dad suffered quite a few hardships, not least when he pursued my mother relentlessly, until she eventually caught him. They were married in 1952, and three days after the wedding, Dad was ordered off to an airbase the North African desert, and didn't see my mother for nearly two years. No wonder it was years after their marriage that I finally came into the world. It explains a lot.

Today, Dad lives alone in a nice house on the edge of Plymouth, with a very large garden, several buzzards and a herd of deer to keep him occupied. He has a passion for gardening and of course, he loves his writing. He will write just anything – short stories, novels, poems, reflections – anything but a cheque.

His memory is still as sharp as ever, even now into his 93rd circuit of the sun. He is writing more than ever, and that blessed iPad is a source of delight to him, and the stuff of nightmare for me (I'm usually the one who has to sort out all the technical issues that seem to crop up regularly).

And here, in your hands right now, you are holding the product of all those hours spent writing. It's a small collection of poems and reflections – which Dad has called *Inspirations*. Collectively, they speak of his greatest love in life. It transcends his passion for gardening and writing, and even trumps his career in the Royal Air Force or his large family. It is even more important dare I say it, than my late mother Ruth, who was, and still is, the love of his life.

No, more important to him than any of these is his personal faith in Jesus Christ – and the transformational power that God has imbued into Dad's life. He's a man of faith and Dad knows exactly where he is headed. One day he will be reunited with my mother in the presence of his Heavenly Father God – all because of the sacrificial death and triumphant resurrection of Jesus, around two thousand years ago on a lonely hillside outside Jerusalem.

So here they are – Dad's thoughts, recollections, and inspirations, liberally laced with some creative literary expression. I am certain you will enjoy Dad's first publication – and that it will be an inspiration…

…and I hope it encourages you to follow Christ too.

Steve Wheeler
July 2020

NB: All of the profits from the sales of this book will be donated to Open Doors, a charity that supports Christians who are persecuted for their faith worldwide.

The Glory of the Cross

Men may paint Christ
but show little of His outward suffering
They cannot paint the love
that flowed from the heart of God
Men may paint the cursed tree
but not the curse of the law that made it so
Man may paint the Christ bearing
the cross to Calvary
But not the Christ bearing
the sins of the world

Man may describe the nails
piercing His sacred flesh
But who is able to describe
the eternal justice piercing
both flesh and spirit?
They may paint the cup of vinegar
which he did not take
But what of the cup of wrath
he drank to its lowest dregs?

They may show the derision of dark forces
But not the darkness
when God turned his back
on His only Son
They may disclose His hands and feet

mangled and pierced
But who can disclose, in one hand
As it were Christ grasping multitudes of souls
ready to sink into ruin
And in the other hand
an everlasting inheritance for them?

They may describe the blood
which freely flowed from His body
But not the waters of life streaming
from the same source
Which is the eternal blessing
available to all mankind
They may paint the crown of thorns he wore,
But not the crown of glory he alone purchased

And who could paint that awful frown
upon the that glorious brow?
It was a frown not for us
but for the enemy of our souls
They cannot paint His voice,
that reached out to heaven
Pleading with the Father on behalf of men
Or that cry of hope, beseeching the lost
to be reconciled to God

His death, a glorious undertaking
conquered multitude of souls
His glory has spread
a light throughout the world
Penetrating into the darkest areas of sin

This is to all mankind
to those who behold His glory
He will receive the gift of eternal life

His wonderful light produces
a powerful effect wherever it shines
Changing the lives of believers
so they become new creatures in Christ
This glory has the power
to melt frozen hearts
To change sinners into saints
and set them apart

It is the light of life
it give energy to the weak
Power to the powerless
it is the force of thunder
yet milder then the
morning dew on tender grass
It is joy unspeakable and full of glory
while here in earth
and an exceedingly great weight
of glory yet to be

A Borrowed Tomb

Once, there was a borrowed tomb,
Where friends did place a man,
into this grave they gently led,
The precious bleeding lamb.

They placed him there in veils of tears
And cried farewell with growing fears
Then homeward went along the road
Where nights darkness did cast it glow.

Sleep that night was hard to find,
For fears and sorry lined their minds,
They dwelt upon that dying frame
The Christ who died a death of shame.

He had come among them
and spoke in wondrous lays,
how he would set the captives free
who sought eternal ways,
but now that loving Saviour
who brought such love and peace.
Lay in a tomb alone
no more His ways to teach.

One such friend was Mary,
for Christ had set her free,

She was at the crucifixion
when they nailed him to a tree.
She had raced up to the tomb
on that cold and dreadful morn.
Her heart has been so heavy with fear
and ways forlorn.

The tomb she found was empty,
the stone was rolled away,
The grave cloths were folded
and in desolation lay.
The tears did flow upon her face,
No hope now for this fallen race.

Through her tears a form she spied,
Sir where have you taken Him, and why?
Then Angels dressed raiment white said,
Whom seek you here among the dead?

In triumph angels' voices rang,
The Christ you seek has risen,
and over yonder stands
For death and the grave
could never hold the sinless Son of Man
For He the Lord has triumphed
over Satan's evil plan.

Mary's sorrowed heart burst
when joy came rushing through,
Of course the Tomb is empty
and all He said was true!

"He has risen!" was her cry,
as she sped upon her way
to proclaim to all the world at large,
"My Lord has risen today!"

Country Lane

I wandered down a country lane,
where sunshine never shone,
and there a lonely man I gleaned
singing an awesome song,
his eyes did rest upon my face,
as he sang such words of grace
it made me smile,
yet it gave me peace,
and caused my heart to race.

The old man dressed in lowly rags,
no shoes upon his feet,
his hair and beard, white as snow
hung down around his cheeks.
The song as lovely as it was,
soon came to an end.
I thought to move away,
but he motioned me to stay.

I joined him on that mossy bank,
sitting by that rugged saint,
I asked him why he sang alone,
in that dark and dismal hole.
He smiled but answered not a care
shivering in the cooling air.

Removing my coat, I gave it to him.
This act of kindness brought a grin.
"You may see this place" he said
"As dark and bleak fading light,
muddy street where natural light
it never shines in this place dank and deep,
yet the precious Son of God abides here
in this Sovereign Keep.

So close your eyes and you will see
the grace of God, beyond belief."
I rose up from the mossy bank
and knelt upon that muddy street,
closed my eyes in humble prayer,
reaching out in deep despair.
All at once I heard music and song,
gracefully around my head did throng
Majestic and inspiring
that gave my soul a blessing.

Opening my eyes I glanced around
and darkness did no more abound.
No longer knelt in mud of old,
but on a street of pure gold,
the mossy bank was now a throne,
and on it sat a man alone.

Clothed in garments pure white,
His face I could not see.
He carried nail prints in hands and feet.
for the whole world to see.

So I knew it was the Lamb of God,
that dwelt with in this place.
I knelt in silent reverence,
until a voice spoke:
"What is your name?"
My name I uttered,
And then the pages fluttered.
"Yes your name is in the book, it's true.
But it seems you are here far too soon.

So you must return to your own time,
and tell them of your find,
a glimpse of heaven you have seen,
it's real, and not a dream."
Suddenly the scene did change,
once again the darkened lane.
No more the street of pure gold
but mud abounding as of old,
the old man I could not see,
upon that bank where the throne had been.

My coat abandoned all forlorn
lay on that bank, no more adorned.

Down through the years, I did as I was told,
preaching to both the young and old,
but few would listen to what I had to say,
so I just carry on in my own way
until I hear that call one sweet day,
where I will walk the streets of gold for aye.

Ken's Dream

While wandering in my dreams last night,
I saw a wall of stones so bright,
it's buttress high and ivy covered,
and there a door, I soon discovered.
It was a door so crudely fashioned,
with heavy oak and iron lashings.
Searching there a crack that I might view
beyond this door that stood so true
when there a handle I did see
and gladly reached so I could free.

I turned that lock and gave a tug
with all my strength but it would not budge,
it would not yield, that door of oak,
but through the door a voice it spoke.
I heard that voice with urgency say
"Knock and it shall be opened today."
I gladly knocked upon that door
as hard as I could bear,
Quite suddenly the door swung
wide open as if upon the air.

Standing there before me
I saw the Son of Man,
He bid me come much closer
with his outstretched nail scarred hand.

I walked toward my Saviour,
my heart was beating fast.
He looked so pure and radiant,
but would the vision last?

His face so sweet and beautiful
just like I thought He'd be,
smiling down at me in loving ways,
that set my spirit free,
Falling down upon my knees
I called to Him to bless,
and felt His warm tender hands
rest gently on my neck,

He said "There are not so many
who knock at my door any more,
they go another way,
they'd rather live in sin's dark ways
than walk the path I've gladly laid.

So take my message to the lost
and tell them of the rugged cross.
How I did die to set men free
if they would only trust in me.
I gave my all not just a part
that mankind might have a purer heart.
So you must be my voice to tell
the truth to them that walk to hell,
that my blood on Calvary's Cross
is still the way for direction lost,
confess your sins believe in me

and eternal heavens you will see.
For on that great and glorious day
I the Lord will draw you away,
to be with me in eternity sweet
where all your loved ones you will meet.
So take my message pass it on
unto the lost in word and song,
sing it from mountains high,
the day of my return is drawing nigh."

Jesus drew near

Two men walked along the dusty road on a long journey, yet to reach their home. Their thoughts were full of danger, remorse, and fear, disappointment overwhelming them at the loss of a teacher held so dear. They walk side-by-side as they recalled events, and what they had witnessed and seen was so intense.

Jesus the healer and leader of men bearing a cross of shame on which life would end. They had watched the Roman soldiers with hammers and with spikes, driving them through the precious hands of Jesus with all their might.

Those very hands that gave wondrous lights to them that walked in darkness never knowing the light. These were the hands that blessed the fish and loaves, to feed five thousand souls, to send them on their way. These were the hands that touched the dead, raised them up to life again, these hand that touch the lepers, healing and giving them new life, were very likely in the crowd following behind so tight.

The atmosphere on that crucifixion day was full of hate and fear, causing all to feel some guilt through the sorrow and tears. Even the governor that day had washed his hands, declaring "I find no fault in this man, so His blood is on your hands, and on your children children's hands."

They raised the cross with our Saviour in the centre, on each side a criminal who was there, they deserved to die, but not this holy man of peace. All so an evil man could be released.

As those two walked in conversation they were interrupted by a stranger drawing near, "What is it causing you such fear?" he asked. They had not noticed the stranger drawing near. "Are you a stranger, and have you not heard, how they have crucified our Jesus, filled the city with fear?"

Jesus gave them a study of history from Moses and the prophets to what had happened on the cross. Later when they arrived at their home, they asked the stranger not to go on alone, but to eat with them at their home. Jesus took the bread and blessed it by lifting it high toward the heavens. Suddenly their eyes were opened, as they saw the nail prints in his hands. It was their blessed Saviour, He has risen as was planned!

Soon the room was empty, only they were there, they would go back out into the night, and walk the road so dark, to tell the disciples that they had seen the master:

He has risen from the dead!

Later they told the disciples, didn't our hearts burn with in us as Jesus revealed the kingdom yet to come?

I Have Come to Take You Home

Hello, are you ready?
I'm here to take you home.
The Father sent me for you,
all you sins have been atoned.
For many years you have been faithful
to God's word alone.

You have spread the gospel message
to many in great need.
You have brought comfort, peace,
shown kindness to those who had been freed.

You have set a good example to all you have met,
who were seeking eternal truth with a past to forget,

Are you ready to go?
Your time on Earth is over,
you have done all that you could,
Your record is good, your reward to hold,
is waiting there, a crown of gold.

Your Father is there on His throne,
ready to welcome his earthly saints home.
You've been washed in the blood of Jesus,
so you're free from guilt and sin.
Are you ready to go?

—

No time for goodbyes,
you are off to see the King
who gave you life anew,
you will meet Him soon it's true,
see Him face to face and tell your story,
saved by grace and in His glory
Are you ready to go?

Minute by Minute...

Every ticking of the clock,
brings each one of us closer
to that moment of death.
Whether we live a long life
or a short one, it matters not,
because we all die.

But it's what we do with
each and every moment,
once that precious moment is gone,
we can't recall it,
or reuse it,
We can't live it again.
so what are we doing
with these precious moments?
Are they being enjoyed?
Used wisely?
Perhaps wasted?
or spent in bed?
Half of our lives are spent in bed,
so half of our lives
are used up in resting
and restoring our bodies.

So when we look at it,
we don't have long here on Earth,

so what are we doing with our time?
Some are raising families,
others are building reputations,
or an education for themselves,
others are spending time enjoying
the pleasure that this life affords.
Others are faithful family members
working hard to supply food and shelter
for their children and love ones.

Do we come under one of these headings?
It matter not which one,
we all have to leave when we receive the call.
We can do nothing to avoid that call,
it will come soon enough.
But we can do something here and now
about living a long life?

Billy Graham, said:
"When you come to my funeral,
I shall be more alive then, than ever I was."
He was so right.
Here on Earth we may be promised
three score and ten
seventy years
some by means of good health,
may be granted longer,
but we all will depart in the end.

You see it's not how we live,
but how we die that decides

where each of us will end up.
The question is where will that be?
It could be in the courts of heaven
with the son of God,
or in the catacombs of Hell
with Satan himself.

It's not very good prospects down there.
When it comes down to brass tacks,
it's a clear case of who we know,
and who know us!
Jesus said, I know my sheep by name.
Is He familiar with your name?

Many make provisions for their loved ones,
when they have passed on,
that's good stewardship.
Yet there was one who made
provision not only for a few,
but for all mankind,
so that we might spend eternity with Him,

His name was Jesus.
He left a long lasting legacy for all mankind,
that if anyone would call upon His name,
Jesus would hear and answer.
And those who called would have
the opportunity
to spend eternity with Jesus in glory.

Yes, every moment is precious to us

so we must live them well.
It only take one moment
to call upon the name of Jesus for salvation.
Where there is a guarantee to anyone
who calls upon the name of Jesus,
that there is a mansion in glory.
Jesus said "I go to prepare a place for you,
that where I am, there you may be also."

Heaven is where there will be no more night,
no more pain,
no more sickness,
no more fear,
no more death,
no more sorrow or tears,
only peace and everlasting Joy.
Remember: it only takes a moment
to call out His name and receive salvation.

Our Plenteous Father

I will pour water on him who is thirsty
I will pour ointment on those who are hurting
I will pour blessings on those that are sorrowful
I will pour liberty to those who are captive
I will pour comfort onto the comfortless
I will pour peace on them in deep sorrow
I will pour healings on those bearing great pain
I will pour deliverance on them who are in bondage
I will pour grace on them that need saving
I will pour hope on those that are suffering
I will pour strength on them that are weak
I will pour love on those that are loveless
I will pour power on those who are struggling
I will pour out my Spirit on those who seek new
vision
I will pour my favour on them without hope
I will breathe my breath into those who are flagging
I will pour joy on them who are sad and lonely
I will pour love on them who are close to death
I will pour out the bread of life, to the hungry
I will endlessly pour benefits from the storerooms of
glory
to those that call upon my name
Who are in need, because I Am that I Am,
The God of graciousness and love

The Days are Drawing to a Close

Days are drawing to a close
the pressures have started to ease.
my body is aching from head to toe
I'm trying so hard to please
I'm finding my life so busy
with the demands upon my time.

Alarm bells ringing, messengers
calling for this and for that.
They won't take no for an answer,
they want miracles, it's as simple as that.

I do what I can with so many demands,
but still they are demanding more
with constant knocking on my door.
When I say oh, please give it a rest,
they shout out you're not doing your best!

They need rain, but demand sunshine bright
they shout back in anger,
you never get anything right!

The demands on my time,
I really don't mind,
but they should be content
with the blessings I've sent.

No one seems grateful for all that I do,
but then I remember my promise to you.
That I would never forsake you,
no matter who you are,
so I still send out my blessings
both near and far.

But now and again
a choice moment I'll have,
when someone sends me a prayer,
not asking or demanding,
but rather a blessing to share.

The thanks rising from a grateful heart
with praise and worship to impart,
offering thanks for all I have done,
in their lives and every one.

I do enjoy such precious moments
that are far and few between,
for praise and adoration
are rarities, it seems.

But when such moments happen,
it fills my heart with joy,
to know that someone loves me still,
with deep feelings they employed.

Few without reservation
will tell me they love me

for all that I have done.
I do my best consider the rest,
and seek to answer their request.

However, there is coming a day
that's not too far away
when the whole world
will bow the knee
and ever tongue will confess,
in prayer and worship to me,
so if you are one of mine,
enjoying fellowship divine.

You are welcome to meet
at my throne of grace,
where we will be face to face

I long to hear you say,
in reverence and praise,
"I love you Lord."

That Night in Gethsemane

Men with evil and wicked hearts
    devised to steal our Lord apart.
While He alone in the garden prayed
    they came upon him weapons displayed.
One among them, a kiss of hate,
    he gave to seal the Saviour's fate.
The kiss, a sign to those in shadows waiting,
    that the man of peace should now be taken.
Those man arrived with swords and staves,
    as though against a thief arrayed.
Daily in the temple they had the right
    but not here in the dead of night,
    like sneaking for a fight.
They took the Lord and led Him away,
    to the high priest's house,
    where He was displayed.

The scribes and Pharisees there assembled
Some feared greatly as their hearts trembled.
Which caused each man to seek within,
    to find an answer to their sin.
The blood of goats had been their sway
    but this man had spoken of another way.
A trial of sorts was held that night
    with all the power of evil might,

---

sought they to kill the Son of Man,
to bring to nought His eternal plan
Upon the cross they hung him high
and soon the darkness filled the sky.
The Roman soldiers quaked with fear –
surely the end of the world was near?
Then a voice was heard, full of pain.
It echoed out across the planes
"It is finished!" was His cry,

He had fulfilled His task on Earth to die.
He gave His all to set men free,
to die upon a rugged tree,
then a silence filled the air.
Those around looked in despair,
no more the crowds did cheer and shout.
They moved away, hearts filled with doubts.
The greatest love the world had known
was there displayed on public show.
There for all the world to see and know,
the only way back to God,
is to look upon the cross of shame,
where God the Father sent His Son
to pay the cost for the sins mankind had done.
His blood will cleanse and purify
even the deepest sin devised.

My God

My God can reach into the highest space
to save a falling star.
He'll place them back where they belong,
My God knows where they are.

My God will go into the deepest hell
to save a soul from sin,
His blood was shed on Calvary,
that all should dwell with Him.
My God, a God of love and grace,
who came to save a fallen race.

Yet more than that to save us all,
when Adam from grace did fall.
He is still the Saviour of the lost,
His precious blood has paid the cost.

To all who call upon His name
He will pardon from their sin and shame.
My God is love abundantly,
so freely bestowing love on all He knows.
Like those who bowed the knee of shame
now serving the King, free from blame.

Have you met my Saviour divine,
who sets men free from sins that bind?

Will you not call upon His name?
He will answer in the same old way,
Oh, what is His name? I hear you cry,
fear not He'll hear you if you try.

He is the Son of God above,
Christ is His name, that man of love,
that evil men nailed to the tree,
He willingly embraced death
to save the lost,
like you and me so don't delay
call on Him today

For Jesus is the truth, the life
and the only way.

Nineveh

Years ago we used to sing a song:

Standing somewhere in the shadows you'll find Jesus,
He's the only one who cares or understands,
Standing somewhere in the shadows you will find Him
and you will know him by the nail prints in his hands.

I can inform you Jesus is no longer standing in the shadows of time. He is no longer standing in the wings of the theatre ready to enter onto the stage.

He is now standing centre stage in the full spotlight of divine grace for all to see and to hear, the Saviour of the world, the only answer to all of our problems.

Jesus is there for all to see, not as an actor or a narrator, but as the representative of the Kingdom of God. He is seeking to warn the whole wide world that time is running out for us, much like the time when Jonah was sent by God to warn the inhabitants of Nineveh about their sinful wicked ways, that they should repent, calling out to the living God for forgiveness or they would be utterly destroyed.

The Holy Word declares the inhabitants of Nineveh heard and heeded the call, and the nation was saved.

Here today is that same warning – repent and turn from your wicked ways, and call upon the name of Jesus while you still have time, because that time is running out. Look around you and see the devastation we have caused to the Earth.

In the Fullness of His Beauty

In the fullness of His beauty
I stood a sinner lost,
would I ever find peace of mind
for years that I had lost?
My ways were sad and lonely
with friends I could not trust.
So to that rugged cross I'll cling
and surrender if I must,
So lost I am of that I'm sure,
but He has paid the cost.
So I'll trust in God with all my heart,
and leave this life of dross.

Our God is full of mercy
He showers us with grace.
He sent his only Son to die
to save a fallen race.
So now I'm bathing in the sunshine
with its warmth upon my face,
and I'm standing in his presence
a sinner saved by grace

The Sunrise will come

This moment never fails to excite my soul
when seeing a sunrise ablaze with gold.
Candy floss clouds, hanging in space,
arrayed in positions of honour and grace,
Earth is warmed by the rays of the sun.
but will soon grow cold, when day is done.

I am impressed with God's display,
His heavenly beauty thus arrayed.
God paints the sky with colours aglow,
to the joy and amazement of all below.

Artists attempt to achieve and paint,
the beauty of God's handiwork daily sent.
Writers try to describe in earthly prose,
the greatness of God, His glories told.
Neither express or copy His beauty,
unless it is done in admiring duty.

Rest your head on pillows of peace.
giving thanks to God the morning greet.
the faithful God sent a true sacrifice.
The sunrise will come and awaken new life.

Thursday Night

Not a cloud in the sky,
nor a tear in my eye,
but a smile on my face is revealed.

Silence abounds,
not even a sound,
only the tick of a clock is found.
No church bells pealing,
for a very good reason –
we all have to stay in our homes.

From my window I stare,
but the street are all bare,
not a soul has come near to my door.

A dog walker will occasionally pass,
but more intent on returning home,
he's thinking, how long will this last?

We only see neighbours on
Thursday nights at eight,
when we have the right
to stand outside and have a friendly debate.

We applaud the NHS,
for the work they do in selflessness.

Doctors and nurses should feel proud,
that they are bearing the load of care,
that has been forced upon them,
a load we cannot share.

Even retired doctors and nurses
have returned to ease the stress
of those unfortunate to have caught
this unseen evil mess
that causes each victim high fever,
and a severe shortage of breath.

They are so brave our heroes of the NHS,
but would we also pass the test?

We are excited to be able to stand outside,
to cheer and shout with pure delight.
It's our way of trying to put things to rights.

They are standing in the heat of the battle,
in a war that they must win,
struggling to find a solution,
should it ever return again.

Everyone has had to play their part
to keep our country clean,
but it's the ones at the front
who are feeling the crunch,
with long hours spent at bedsides
nursing problems that are unseen.

So that's why we meet on a Thursday night,

and publicly show our thanks,
when we remember the cost,
that they have paid
in this long bitter battle of loss.

The Atonement

The cross
of Christ
is an object
of such
incomparable
brightness
that it spreads
all its glory
around it to every nation of the earth, all the corners of the
universe, all the generations of time, and all the ages of
eternity. It was the greatest human action and the most
singular and momentous event that ever happened on
Earth, filled as it
was with
splendour
and influence
but in one
moment of
time, and in
a single point
of space.
The splendour
of this great
object fills
immensity
and eternity
with the glory
of God's love.

The sun sets, the sun rises

Glory, glory, glory
at the setting of the sun
We see the handiwork of God
when our daily toil is done

Glory, glory, glory
at the rising of the sun
throughout the day its glory shines
upon the Earth below
to cast its radiance far and wide
the weather it bestows

At the rising of the Sun
revealed God's sovereignty
across the endless skies,
magnificently

For all the world His love to share
there is none other can compare
Few can watch the
glorious setting of the sun
and not behold its beauty
when its task for us is done

Do we ever tell the Lord
how we appreciate the setting sun
or in the early morning

when are day as just begun
that we are very grateful
for the warmth upon our face
and for the brightness of the morning
and the portion of his grace

Imagine, there being no sun at all
No more light, no more warmth
just a cold dark landscape forever more
Now you can see why we should
gave thanks unto the Lord

Beautiful in every way

She is so, so beautiful,
Beautiful in every way
She is so, so beautiful
she stole my heart today.
It's her movement and her grace
that sets my heart to race.
Striding tall and proud
as she moves among the crowds.

I don't even know her name,
but then it's always been the same.
I'm far too shy to say hello
so my love she'll never know.
In the street when she passes by,
she must surely hear my sigh
as my soul screams out in pain
that I may never see her once again
so I'll shall love you from afar
Never knowing who you are.

You will always be it seems
brightly shining through my dreams.

I wrote this some years ago, when a contestant on the TV told the panel of judges he was 28 but had never kissed a girl, or had a girlfriend, because he was so shy, I think his name was Paul Potts. I felt so sorry for him, so I wrote this poem.

Thinking of Home

I came to this promised land of endless sun
and golden sands far across the sea,
sometimes I feel so sad I left
 my homeland of Devon cream teas,
my Cornish relatives and friends,
just across the stream,
I often hear them speak to me
 in my troubled dreams.

How I love my childhood days,
when we would all spend the days
running through the rolling surf,
the sea spray in our face and hair
like a gift of Holy grace.

The Cornish pasties eaten
hot or cold it mattered not,
it was a pleasure just to hold
and to give thanks we were told.
To sink one's teeth into
clotted cream on scone
it's a joy unknown
Till it's been done,
and if you have room
a Cornish ice cream
on the journey home.

The long weary walk
to the station to board the train,
that carried us over Brunel's bridge
 to the coast of Devon and home,
to Plymouth or Devonport station,
it all seemed like a dream,
until you feel the still damp costumes
and the sand and your shoes,
sand that was left in the bath
when the water had been used.

We children would spend
the whole day away,
with no fear or alarm,
we would each watch out for each other
seeing we came to no harm.

I still dream of my childhood
and there are times I can still
smell and taste of the sea,
and hear the screech of the gulls alarm,
as they dive and soar over the sea.

I love the visions I have in my head
of Plymouth Hoe, the wide Sound,
the breakwater beyond
the lighthouse on the Hoe,
and the Moors where I would roam.

I love my West Country
it is where I was born,

I can still shed a tear.
When I look into the past,
of the graves of my parents,
of family members I still miss,
from days when we were young
and the joy that we possessed.
Where life is so much slower,
and our hearts were at peace.
I long to hear that Devonshire burr,
that draws me away to a cove or a bay,
where fishermen sing at the end of the day
when washing their nets,
and cleaning their boats,
The thought of it still
sends a thrill down my spine.
I long to recall those nights long ago
when the whole family gathered
around a log fire aglow,
we would hear the
precious stories of many years ago
that only us *Janners would listen to
and want to know.
There is nowhere like my home,
and one day I hope to see once again.

*Janner – A person who comes from Plymouth

Glory and Fame

Seek not for Glory,
seek not for fame,
but seek knowledge and honour
it's surely worth the gain.
It's for soldiers to win arms to bear,
and to wear medals of glory,
fame is for actors on stage and on screen,
entertaining the public
for applause so it would seem.

All are seeking glory and fame,
while through it all a living to obtain.
Authors and writers do delight
in their craft of telling stories
hoping for a best seller at last.
Many still live, who died long go,
we see them on screens
and on old TV shows,
recover from old rusty reels I suppose.

Some we remember from in books
having done some wondrous deeds
of battles fought-many years ago.
One great leader Churchill describe them as
that British bulldog breed.
Some are ever present in ink on pages of a book,

like Admiral Nelson and the Duke of Wellington
for what they had done.
Each year we lift them up with pride
for the victories they had won.

Honour is for doctors and surgeons,
and men of the cloth,
for professors, teachers, judges,
lawyers and men of the Cross.
For all who are employed in education
Police and law enforcement,
Mayors and council leaders
We all have a slot to fill
in the area where we abide,
To make it a place where
we can walk safely with pride,
knowing we are safe and honoured
and nothing is denied.

But it's only when we are all agreed
that our streets and safe and free from fear,
when we hold our Heavenly Father near,
We have to give the honour
to teachers for the work they do,
It's far better to have honour and knowledge,
that will create glory and fame anew.

Promises

May all our thoughts and
deeds be pure and holy
As we proclaim to the world
His Gospel boldly.
May all we meet be pleased,
greeting us with a smile
with a hug to enfold us
which will carry us for miles.

May our gazing into heaven,
seen through the finest lace
Soon to see the glories of
Christ's redeeming grace.
May all we say and do,
be a blessing to others
with words of encouragement
to children and mothers.

May our walk be straight
and narrow like a farmer ploughs a field
Walking in the furrows
that he has just revealed
May all we hear be pleasing
to our souls, and captivating
and engaging us upon our journey
that is yet to unfold

May all our prayers be
answered with pure delight
As we seek blindly to reach
into Heaven's eternal light.
May all our aches and pains
be instantly healed
As we give thanks to the Father
for victories revealed.

May our promises never be broken,
it is why the Father
left a rainbow in the sky
as a never ending promise.
May our love always be
sincere and rewarding
aiding poor and needy as
with care help employing.

May our hearts overflow
with a glory unknown
mercy given by our God
in measureless tone.
Telling of His glories,
each day bestowed
on sinners like us,
His mercies to unfold.

May our days be long
with a smile and a song
praising our a Saviour

all the day long.
How can we but not love
and adore Him exulting his name
When Jesus shouted down
through space and time
"Father forgive them!"
He had you on his mind.

My Morning Prayer

I awoke this morning with a full and grateful heart,
pleased to have another day, to spend on this earth,
alone yet never apart.

This morning in my prayers I thanked my Heavenly
Father for another day of life in his care, with pain,
but oh the gain, of a wonderful memories I can freely
share. Recalling treasure times again, of precious
moments I have lovingly retained.

In my mind to see the beauty of my wife and friend,
as I gazed into her eyes at our wedding, when she
took my name. When I think of God's daily blessing,
poured over me, my heart is full of gratitude, for His
never endless love to me.

I was praying to Him this morning that I feel His
presents with me every moment of the day.
Sometimes I walk not knowing which way to go,
until I hear his gentle voice whisper the safest path I
should stroll. He is my constant companion where
ever I may roam, He is my guide and comforter, one
day He will lead me safely home.

More to Follow

Many years ago when I use to preach, I was asked to give a talk about Heaven, not a subject any of us can freely speak on. We can only give what we read in the pages of the Bible. But I told a few stories I had heard about what others had experienced in this particular realm, during their ministry.

One story was of the pastor who was visiting an elderly sister. She did not have long left on this Earth. He spent time with her, reading the word and reassuring her that all would be well. She said, "would you promise me something pastor, you will do one more thing for me?"
"But of course my dear, what is it?" he replied
"Would you see I have a spoon I'm my hand when I die?"
"Why would you're want me to put a spoon in your hand?" He asked.
"Well, whenever we had a church meal, you would always say: 'Keep you spoon, because there is more to follow'."

She was a woman of expectation, she had enjoyed this life down here, but she was looking forward to something far better in the glory. She didn't want to miss out on what was waiting upon her arrival into the presence of her Lord and Saviour.

Another story was of a well-to-do man in the church, he had heard of a dear pastor who had to give up his ministry through ill health. He had no income and was living in poverty. The rich man found his old pastor's address, and put a large sum of money in an envelope. He was about to seal it, when the thought came to his mind. Knowing the old pastor, he knew if he received a large sum of money, he would give some of it away to help others.

So the wealthy man sent just a small amount in the envelope with a note saying "More to follow." There is a great lesson there in that little story. We may struggle down here with life, but our Redeemer and Lord is sending just enough to keep us going, knowing we may give it away or waste it. There is always more to follow, not only in this life, but if we belong to Jesus, there is so much more to follow on the other shore. There is the joy of seeing our loved ones again, who have gone before us. They will be there to greet our arrival in eternity.

Then we have that powerful moment that we have been talking and preaching about all our lives, since the scales fell from our eyes, when we saw the light of salvation. We will see the face of Jesus our Lord. Face to face we will behold Him, and it will be worth it all when we see Jesus! Heaven is a wonderful place, but our interest will not be Heaven, or the beauty it possesses. Our focus will be on the One who made it possible for you and I to be there, the One who said, I go to prepare a place for you, that where I am, there you shall be also.

That is Jesus, the lover of my soul. Yes friends, there is more to follow. Much more then we could possible imagine. And if you don't yet have that assurance, then you need to speak to someone soon, to make a discussion for Christ blessings to you all. Here is a short prayer you can pray:

Dear God, I'm sorry for my sins and I invite you to come into my life. Please forgive me, cleanse me from my sin and assure me of a place with You in Heaven. I ask this in the name of Jesus, who died in my place. Amen.

Don't Delay

Are you worried and troubled about anything,
wondering and fearing what tomorrow will bring?
If you are longing to tell someone you feel all alone,
but your friends are all burdened with cares of their
own,

there is only one place,
and only one friend,
who is never too busy,
on whom you can depend.

Where can you seek Him and find Him today?
At the altar of prayer – go there now, don't delay.

There are no borders

I had a message from a lady I have known from my youth, who lived in Hong Kong for many years. She mentioned in passing that she had seen an archway, with these words above it:
"There are no borders East is east and west is west, and never the twain will meet,"
There were two men pictured beneath, grasping hands. At once I had an image form in my mind. "I can write a poem about that," I said. She replied "Oh please do, Ken." So here it is:

There are no borders, east or west
north or south, that can stand the test,
where determined men are standing
face-to-face from different worlds, apart
with love for freedom deeply
embedded within their hearts,
speaking a language neither understand,
but with friendly smiles upon their face so true,
will wipe away the hate they knew.

It's not yours or mine, but for all to share,
that look and stare in deep despair,
or someone boasting and shouting in the air.
It's all mine, all mine.
It's only his for sure when he has been
buried beneath the floor,
for a long, long time.

There are no borders, East or West,

—

North or South that will stand the test,
of freedom loving people seeking a better life,
education for their children,
healthcare for the wife,
employment for the husband,
seeking peace, avoiding strife.

The whole world sees on the TV,
that life is better in the West.
We have walked for many months,
they say, over deserts, hills, and plains,
seeking to find that place
where our troubles end,
and a new beginning in our lives,
on which we will now depend.

We arrived at borders,
but we are turned away.
So we go and rest, then go back
and try another way.
Some of the guards have
friendly smiling faces,
we think they will let us in.
But without the right papers,
we have only ourselves to blame.
Can they not see we are weary,
hungry, and afraid,
no one comes to help us,
in these sad and fearful days.

However, two ladies came our way.

They gave us food and water,
they stayed with us to
comfort, help, and pray.
"That border is stopping you
from crossing into that land.
But it is not theirs to own,
it was created and made by God's own hands.
Who suffered and died alone
for your sins His blood has now atoned.
If you give your heart to Jesus,
He will remove all of life's borders
so you will have no trouble entering Heaven.

There are no guards up there,
only friendly smiling angels
greeting you with a grin,
"Welcome home, dear saints!" they'll cry,
"Your friends and love ones
are already safely inside."

A Tribute to my Beautiful Ruth

When the light of this world
is losing its lustre
and the strength of the sun grows weak

When the cold hand of death
has issued its threat
And there is no more coming of spring

Then the light of your soul
will break forth again
and blossom like a rose

The warmth of your love
will heat the cold earth
and cause your beautiful to unfold

For the sound of your singing
the smile of your face
will cause a new dawn to awaken
and the sunshine it brings will herald a spring
which was never seen by our race

For your soul to me, will never diminish
and your beauty will always remain

No darkness will ever over shadow you there

Your beauty will drive it away
In my mind I still see your beautiful face
The beauty that captured my soul
your hair so perfect, arranged with great care
led me to levels unknown

Purity

Purity, O Purity,
my Saviour died in purity,
like gold that passes through the flame
or rain drops falling earth to gain.
They nailed him to a rugged tree
that I might dwell in purity
my captive spirit free at last
to shun the evils of my past,
to walk with pride the streets of home.
now free am I, my spirit roams.

The world around now seems so bright
since I have found His wondrous light.
His words of love so rich to me
with daily grace supplies each need.
Jesus who saved me by his grace,
one day to see His wondrous face.
His joy each day on me bestow,
is some times more than I can hold.

Rhythm

The mystery of rhythm in the soul,
and how it got there, no-one seems to know.
Even little children with no words of knowledge,
will smile and jig to clapping hands or someone
singing a tune.

If we went to other nations,
heard the rhythms that they sing,
it's no too different from our own.
But the question is, where does it come from
when it's not just ours alone?

I believe it's in the body of everyone,
placed there for each of us to know
that the God who first made man,
gave us rhythm in our souls
for all on earth to sing.

Glory to God in the highest
who loves to hear his people sing,
raising praise and adoration
to the glory of the King.
He gave a beat to our heart within us,
pumping the rhythm of life.
It's the first thing that a baby hears
inside the mother's womb,

the rhythm of her heartbeat
as it beats an healthy tune.

So that is where I believe rhythm comes from –
it's the beating of the heart,
once we are without that rhythm,
we will very soon depart.

Coronavirus

We have been instructed to stay in our homes,
And not to mix with others but just stay alone.
This virus appears quite harmless,
because the germs we cannot see.

But don't be fooled, it's out there,
and its danger you may feel
It's waiting its evil germs to employ,
on the weakest and oldest lives to destroy.

The virus is in the air
and in the lungs of others to share,
Silently lying in wait ready its evil
to add to our deep despair.

So many appear reckless and unafraid,
yet still breathing God's fresh air
and thinking they have the right.
We will all have to pull together
doing what we are told,
not doing our own thing,
if we should be so bold.

But a suggestion I would make,
to win this awful war,
we should be spending more time
on our knees praying to the Lord,

To help us in our time of need Father,
we have never needed you more.
We are so weak in this desperate situation.
It's God's strength and grace we need,
and a deeper revelation.

The blessings I have received
from the Lord are far more than I need.
So I will pass them on to others,
blessing to my loved ones I leave.

Things we Loved as Children

Play cost us very
little at all
a length of rope
a tennis ball
A whip and a top
a fag card or two
skip and a hop
some chalk would do
A hoop and a stick
a few silly tricks
With a stop me and buy one
all shard-a-lick down to the beach
where we all had a dip
We laughed and played
till the tide came in
If I had a penny
I felt just like king

We'd run to the shop
or go to the flicks
contented with very little
all in the same boat
If it was raining
we would tell a few jokes
Penny comics were something to treasure
In their pages we found
so many pleasures

Cowboys and Indians
we'd play after tea
Ending the evening
singing songs of glee
Red sails in the sunsets
a favourite to sing
We'd croon together
like a singer called Bing
There was a gas light
at the top of the street

When it was dark
that's where we'd meet
We'd play tag and bulldog
nobody had a care
We were all thrown together
our burdens to bear
Then a shout from father
"It's time for bed!"
Then off to our homes
we would joyfully head

If it were Saturday
we'd have good bath
It hung on the wall
made of zinc and brass
Filled from the copper
it really was quite hot
We were bathed by older sisters
a heavy handed lot

They would push our heads under
rub us till we were raw
Throw us one to the other
no thoughts taken at all

We would sit by the fire
to hear the wireless set
Dad would twiddle the knobs
a station to select
We would hear the atmospheric
coming over the air
We would put our fingers in our ears
giggle in despair

We would huddle close together
sitting back to back
hearing that whispering voice,
"Here is the Man in Black."
Every week this would scare us,
but still we asked for more.

One night we heard
a knocking at the door,
we children screamed and ran about
not knowing what to do.
It turned out to be the coal man,
requesting his dues

We never seemed unhappy
or short of things to do
We had the street to play in,

no traffic threatened you.

We couldn't wait for Sunday school
to hear the Bible stories
We'd sit with mouths wide open
startled by its glories.
Sometimes we were unruly,
not behaving as we ought.
Hearing of the battles
the courage that they fought.

But they taught us good from evil,
and others to respect,
That Jesus loved the whosoever,
we were each given a text.

Today's children have so much,
yet still they ask for more.
They sit for hours at play stations,
then say Mum – I'm bored!

Burning Embers

A father and his son were out walking through the city streets, when the son suddenly stopped, turned and asked his father,

"Father, why is our city so empty, and so deserted? I was told it once a great city so busy, full of people."

"Why are there so few people, and why are so many shops boarded up? I was told this was once the greatest city in our nation. But it's nothing more now than a backwater, empty of life."

"Why is that, Father?"

The father replied, "Because the people turned their faces away from the living God, and when the plague came, they failed to call on His name for healing."

"That is so sad," said the son, "to think that this city was once a vibrant, thriving metropolis, but it's now only burning embers."

Autumn

The Autumn of life is a troubling time,
when movements are slower
and eyesight becomes less fine.
I lived a good life with my precious wife,
with children so bright, that bound us so tight,
with happiness, contentment,
and endless delights.

We worked well together,
our life was a dream.
but one day our dear wife
and mother had to leave.
We wept as a family,
saying goodbye to our queen.
We have memories we cherish
of moments so sweet
like a day out in the car,
that were always a treat.

My mind is a treasury
filled with such times –
the blessings we shared,
are now in heaven sublime.
I can recall such precious memories
again and again,
they never diminish

they are always the same.
God gave me Ruth,
to love and to hold,
I have such moments,
I find hard to bestow.

We shed tears together,
when I had to depart,
my duties called me off
to foreign parts.
I still miss Ruth,
we are never really apart,
while the Lord gives me breath
and a beating heart

I still have my treasured memories
sealed up for so long
God has allowed me to retain them
to keep my spirit strong.
to fortify me when I'm feeling low,
when nights are long and sleep won't flow.

Until the day that I'm called home,
where I see my Jesus on His Throne.
No longer on the cross of shame
but in the Glory, praise His name.
Until that day that I am called
I will be singing He is Lord of All.

God Provides

I served in the Royal Airforce as a chef for over 32 years. In the early 70s I was seconded to the NATO forces, where I was based in the South of The Netherlands in a city called Maastricht. My family came with me and during our time there, we made friends with an American missionary called Tom, his wife Nancy and their family, who attended the same church.

Now it seems odd talking about missionaries in a developed country like Holland, but they were there, and a number of them there were living just like any other family in the city. Tom's income was provided by a church back in the United States, but at that time things were not going well on the foreign currency exchange for the US Dollar. Its value had dropped significantly since they had first arrived, so their income was gradually becoming less and less.

I had no knowledge of this at that time, until another English member of our congregation approached me to ask me how much money we had in the church fund. I was the treasurer of our church fellowship, we had a fair amount, so he suggested that we could help out Tom and Nancy by buying some food for them, rather than simply giving them money. So I mentioned this to my wife, Ruth and we agreed to help. The following Saturday I went with Ruth to the NAAFI, our service shopping store, and we started to fill a shopping trolley with provisions.

Ruth was the wise one and she managed the task from a woman's perspective – yes to that item, no to others. We spent more than two-hundred Dutch Guilders, the currency of the Netherlands before the Euro was in circulation. At the time a British pound could be exchanged for about eight Guilders and this kind of money would go a long way.

We filled the rear of our car, which had a big boot and more space on the back seat. We then drove to the camp where the church meetings were held. After the service we were enjoying our English tea and it had grown quite dark by this time. I waited till everyone was talking and eating and then went across to speak to Tom.

"I need to show you something Tom, it's downstairs" I said. We walked down the stairs and outside into the night air. I was parked right next to his eight seater Dormer van.

"Open the back of your van, Tom." I said.
"What for?" He asked, with a puzzled look.

I opened the boot of my car, which was packed with items of food and Tom just stood there rooted to the spot and stared.

"Are You alright Tom?" I enquired. I could just about see from the security lights that he was crying, I thought it was gratitude that we were helping him and his family.

But it was much more than that. After a time, Tom pulled himself together and was able to speak again.

"We had nothing in the house to eat when we left this evening, so as a family we got down on our knees, and asked the Lord to be so gracious as to fill our kitchen with food, and you come along bringing all this food, it is a miracle of God Grace, He has answered our prayers, thank you my Father and my God."

When I heard that, I was shocked to think that Ruth and I had been part of God's plan and that we should be used in a miracle. That God the Father had used us to be part of that miracle reduced me to tears. It was such a humbling experience, the two of us clung to each other. We filled his van with the provisions, and even had to use part of the back seats to get it all in.

When we went back upstairs Tom told Nancy what had happened, and then she started crying. Then the children wanted to know why their parents were weeping, and soon it was spreading like a forest fire.

Soon everyone was crying with joy because of the goodness of God's love. One of God's names is *Jehovah Jireh* – meaning God provides. It's not every day you feel elated with the joy of the Lord, but when you realize that you have been used by God to bring peace and happiness into someone else's life, I tell you – it's transforming, and extremely humbling.

South Sea Islander

This is a reworking of an old story that I read several years ago. I had almost forgotten about it. It was a about south sea island chief, who had sailed to another island far away from his own island to trade. It was while he was there that he met a captain of a steam ship that traded among the many remote islands in that part of the South Seas. That day they happily passed the time of day together. As they parted the captain agreed to call in to the chief's island the next time he was in the area.

The captain was concerned about the old chief and his crew being lost at sea. There are no signposts in the ocean and the boat they rowed seemed flimsy. So he gave the chief his own personal compass, to help him find his way home. The old chief thanked him, and said "I will give it back to you when you visit my island."

Before departing for home, the chief hung the compass on a piece of string around his neck. The crew armed with their paddles, rowed out into the vast sea. It had taken them 13 hours of paddling, so he assumed it would take 13 hours to return home. They could do nothing till the stars appeared in the heavens, then they would know where they were. However low clouds now obscured the stars, and they had no way of knowing where they were, or which direction to take, so they stopped for a rest.

The chief put one hand on the compass and with his other hand pointed to the heavens. When they started paddling again, he changed the course, staying on that heading, until one of the crew shouted, land ahead!

Another hour and they were on the beach of their island where everyone was there waiting to welcome them home. It was a few weeks later that the steam ship was seen from the watch tower. The islanders sent their boats out to bring the visitors ashore. On the first boat back to shore was the sea captain. He was pleased to see the old chief safe and sound.

"So you got back alright Chief, the compass was a big help to you was it?" "Oh yes," came the reply "When we could not see where we were going, I put my hand on the compass and my other hand pointed to the heavens, and I said, 'Great Father would you please show me the way to our Island!' The moment I did so, a warm wind blew against the left side of my face, so I turned the boat in that direction, keeping the warm wind blowing on my back. In a short while there we were, with the island directly in front of us. Thank you Captain for lending me your precious charm."

He took the compass – the 'charm' – from around his neck, and handed it back. The captain smiled but said nothing. God has His own ways of proving his worth, and his Glory. Within a matter of months a missionary had been sent to that Island, and soon after a Christian church had been established.

Prodigal Child

This is a story I was told by a man who lived near a beach on the North Cornwall coast. The event took place on the sands of the holiday town of Newquay.

The man had been walking his dog early in the morning when he noticed a man fully dressed running into the sea. Guessing that something unusual was taking place, he raced toward the man. As he got closer he saw the man again, and he was now carrying what looked like a child out of the sea in his arms. By the time he got to the man, he saw it was a boy of about five or six years old. The rescuer was working furiously on the lad.

The man who told me this story said he watched the man who was wet through, working hard as he performed external cardiac massage on the lads chest, but nothing was happening. Soon it was clear the lad was not responding to the action of the man's desperate efforts.

"Give it up mate, he's gone, you're wasting your time!" a bystander said. The man working on the lad took no notice, but he was now showing signs of flagging.

"You've done your best mate, now is the time to stop." repeated the bystander. With that the man stopped pumping the boy's chest long enough to gasp "Would you stop, if this was your son?"

This was a shock to the bystander. Realising the man was the boy's father, he moved him gently to the side, got down on his knees and began pumping on the lads chest himself, telling the father to breathe into his child's mouth. When he saw the young lad begin to revive, the bystander wept, realising he had told the father to stop.

Many years later that same bystander explained that he had a son of his own, who had gone off the rails, becoming involved in drug abuse. He warned his son that if he didn't change his ways, the young man would have to leave their home.

The son duly left and made his way to London. This broke his mother's heart, but every night she would pray for her son's safe return. The father also thought about that little lad on the beach, whose father would not give up, so together the mother and father prayed continuously for their sons safe return.

One day he did return after seven long years, but not alone, he had a wife and two babies, they had been faithful just like that lad on the beach whose father would never give up. Neither did he and his wife.

If you have a prodigal child, don't give up on them, keep praying in the name of Jesus for their safe return, and the God of miracles will honour your faithfulness and bring them home.

And please also remember this: God, our Heavenly Father has never given up on you.

Dumping Ground

I'm 92 years old, I've lived a long life and I've seen a lot of this world.

A few years ago I had an road accident while out driving. I wasn't badly injured but my car was a write-off. Both my sons came to me afterwards and suggested that perhaps it was time to stop driving.

I've not had another car since. As a consequence of losing my car, my garage is now a dumping ground for rubbish and abandoned items. It's in quite a mess and someday someone is going to have to clean it out, which won't be a simple task.

The truth, that just like my garage is a dumping ground for rubbish, so I used to have a heart and soul that were in a similar state. They were full of sin, evil and despair, and no one wanted to come near me.

One day, I had had enough, I could bear it no more, and there was only one thing left to do. I gave my heart and life to the Lord Jesus, and became a Christian.

Now my previously cluttered soul is clean and tidy, and guess what, I didn't have to do any of the work. One day it was there, the next day it was clean and spotless.

God did a spring clean on me and I've never regretted it since.

Have you got a cluttered soul, that needs attention, or do you feel your life has become unpleasant? If you do, then try handing it all over to Jesus.

His precious blood and righteousness will make it clean and pure once again.

Surprise Visit

I was laying in my bed alone, and suddenly it felt as though someone else was in the room. I looked around but none was found, I drew the curtains to let the moon light in, and there

I saw a bunch of fresh tulips neatly lying, and on the petals two tear drops I saw drying, I know not why they were there, and who had left them for me

Perhaps it was my dear mother, who had died so long ago, she was paying me a visit, her tears there to show, that she still loved and missed me, she wanted me to know.

He took my sins and my sorrows

He took my sins and my sorrows
He suffered and died alone,
His precious blood now atoned,
He made me whiter than snow.
He did it by willing going to Calvary's cross,
They thought the devil had won,
and that Jesus had lost
But they had yet to count the terrible cost.

Three days and nights long
they waited in fear and tears,
but the coming days of rejoicing
was drawing very near.
When they got to the tomb,
the stone was moved.
What would they have done
with His body so soon?
Where have they taken him,
and where has he gone?

"Please tell me, what have you done
to Gods own Son?
Mary pleaded in defeated tone,
as she stood there all alone.
"If you're looking for Jesus,
you won't find him in there.

He is not far from you,
he standing just over there,"

Through her tears of sorrow,
she saw the man of peace.
He was no longing in the grave,
but dressed in garments neat.
"Mary stop your weeping, everything's alright."

She knew the voice of her master,
no longer behind a stone.
The grave could not hold him,
his body to the Earth only loaned.
She went then to tell the others,
that were waiting there in fear.

"I have come with good news,
so you can wipe away your tears
The master is no longer in the grave,
He has risen! We no longer need to fear."

I had a friend who needed to undergo a serious operation for cancer.
He told me he was very fearful, so I wrote this poem for him.

The Lord is my Shepherd

The Lord is my Shepherd, I did cry
repeated it again and again as I
was pushed on a trolley
toward the theatre doors,
Suddenly my fears were gone
I no longer felt alone
Someone was there beside me
to comfort and atone

Those words that I had heard
so many years ago
spoke peace and blessings
into my very soul

The more I said those word of love
the more my fears were freed
The Lord is my shepherd,
I shouted out loud
I wanted the whole world to hear,
of the one who gave His life for me
And who was driving away my fears

The surgeons did a first class job,

they managed to cut it away
But it was the power of prayer
that none can compare

So I thank my Lord,
helping the surgeons the pressure to bear
I don't suffer so much with worries and fears,
I simply don't give a care

Now I'm spending my time
counting my blessings
I don't have the time
for empty confessions

I can still feel the Lord's blessings
and the peace that He gave
at that time when my thoughts
and blessing were grave
my Jesus who died to give us
mercy and peace,
has still the power
to set men free
from the burden of sin
and set us at liberty
from death and the grave

Ascent Love

She was not a woman of powder or paint,
but a face of pure beauty with a touch of holy grace.
It thrilled my soul that she processed such charm,
that burned within this heart of mine.
Her heart was full of loving grace,
that cast its glory into space,
it made me want to embrace
the lovely beauty of her face.

I saw such a beautiful lady in my church,
my eyes were constantly on the alert,
to see if she would look my way
or was this not just another day.
I knew in a moment my heart cried out
this is the one, there is no doubt,
She has the face of an angel,
of that I am sure there is no need
to go searching, around anymore,

I won her heart, yes wedding bells rang,
my dreams all came true,
the union was grand,
she was always a sight to gladden the heart,
I wanted to love her with all my heart,
but sadly I had to depart, away on a troopship to
foreign parts

Many years have passed,
but never did time steal,
nor harm the beauty of girl of mine,
her glowing face shone with the beauty of Jesus
her saviour divine
and radiated like pure gold

No longer now do I withhold,
that face that caused my heart to race
is now gone to a far better place.

The world around is now so dull
without her beauty to unfold,
but in my mind I have her still
if only in my dreams until in heaven,
when I too reach those golden shores to see her
beauty standing there,
where we will be together ever more.

Precious Moments

Sitting alone in my room,
I've just enjoyed
my lunch of chicken noodles,
and to follow apple strudel
with clotted cream employed,
a cup of coffee near at hand,
I'm gazing out across the land
from my window at nothing in particular,
just the row of housing,
and cars upon their drives.

But what a precious moment where nothing is
moving, not even the trees all is lifeless, not even a
breeze.

The only sound I hear is music playing near, that is
adding pure pleasure to this moment I hold dear.

There are no birds or animals,
nothing in my gaze no sound I hear,
only the scratching my pen,
as it moves across the page.
It's like someone else is writing,
I'm just holding the pen.

I have no fear or concern, but I want this precious
moment to linger in my way so I can recall it, on
another day.

No one else is here to enjoy these
precious moments of mine,
only the sun rays falling on to this scene of time,
there is no one
and nothing to disturb
this moment of grace.
Such precious moments
are few and far between.

I have the feeling all is well,
my soul is at rest,
contentment to dwell
in a haven of peace.

Eternal Thanks

I awoke this morning
with a full and grateful heart
Pleased to have another day
to spend upon this Earth
Alone yet never apart
This morning in my prayers
I thanked my Heavenly Father
for another day of life in his care
With pain, but oh the gain
Of wonderful memories
I can freely share

Recalling treasured times again
Of precious moments
I have lovingly retained
In my mind to see
the beauty of my wife and friend
As I gazed into her eyes
on our wedding day
the day she took my name

When I think of God's daily blessings
poured out on me
My heart is full of gratitude
For his never ending love for me
In my prayers to Him this morning

I feel the presence with me
every moment of the day
Sometimes I walk not knowing
which way to go
I will hear His gentle voice whisper
the safest pathway I should stroll

He is my constant companion
wherever I may roam
He is my guide and Comforter
and I know that one day
He will lead me safely home

Sunrise

The moment never fails to excite my soul
When seeing a sunrise ablaze with gold
Candy floss clouds hanging in space
Arrayed in a position of honour and grace
Earth is warmed by the rays of the sun
It will soon grow cold when the day is done

I am impressed with God's display
His heavenly beauty thus arrayed
God paints the sky with colours aglow
To the joy and amazement of all below
Artists attempt to achieve in paint
The beauty of God's handiwork daily sent

Writers try to describe in earthly prose
The greatness of God his glories told
Neither express or copy his beauty
Unless it is done in admiring duty

Rest your head on pillows of peace
Give thanks to God the morning to greet
The faithful God sent a true sacrifice
The sunrise will come and awaken new life

In the Hands of the Potter

When a skilled potter presses his hands into the clay it presses right back, giving him some indication of what he is able to make with that particular lump of clay. He can determine if it will hold together or if it will be of no use.

I have to tell you that when God chose us He knew what each of us was capable of doing, whether we will hold together or fall apart. He knew at once what he could make from each one of us. And He seeks to make each of us into a perfect copy of His Son Jesus.

Whenever a potter makes something, he will stamp his maker's mark onto it so everyone can see who made it. And by the same token, if we are made into something by God, we will have His stamp on our lives. If we are His the stamp will read: 'Born again'.

Loved Ones

As one grows older, there are sadly more funerals to attend. When I think of all the loved ones and friends I have seen lying in their coffins, I often wonder if someone ever forgot to tell them that they loved them. Or did someone never tell them how much they were appreciated while they were still alive? Were they commended for their faithfulness, or commitment, or for their hard work?

Were they thanked for their positive attitude toward their family, or their total involvement with their friends? If they were not told, I would think, it is now too late. They are gone from this world.

I once heard a man weeping on the radio, because his father had never told him he loved him. Do you owe someone a word of thanks or appreciation for something they have done or said? Don't put it off any longer. Call them today and tell them because tomorrow may be too late.

I was conducting a funeral of an elderly lady several years ago. I knew nothing about her or her family, but the lady she was staying with told me she was a Christian.

As it turned out, she had half a dozen children, each with their own families. They were all assembled at the crematorium to pay their final respects.

Sadly none of them had much to do with their mother, each too busy with their own lives. I knew none of this until after the funeral.

When everyone had entered into the memorial chapel, and all had settled into their seats, I welcomed them.

Then I walked over to the casket, put my hand on the lid and said "All of you gathered here, whether relations or friends of this dear departed soul – it is now too late to say your goodbyes, it's too late to say 'I love you Mum'."

At that moment I thought that World War Three had broken out. There was sobbing, moaning, screaming as people wept, fell on the floor and hugged each other in tears, trying to seek some solace. It was utter chaos.

This was a consequence of the family neglecting to be with their mother. They had left it too late to tell her they loved her, or to show their appreciation or affection. For the rest of their days they would now have to live with this burden of unrest.

I have conducted many funerals but this one was the most difficult. I have never seen an entire family suffer under such conviction. In never discovered the reason they had abandoned their mother for so many years, but I did witness first-hand the pain and suffering that it left behind. It was not a comfortable experience for anyone.

So if you love someone, please don't leave it too late to tell them you care.

The Desert Well

Oh the deep, deep love of Jesus. Deep calleth unto deep at the noise of the water spout: all the waves and billows are gone over me.

Come with me back to a time in the 1950s when I was stationed in Libya, in the North Africa desert. I was based in a Royal Air Force (RAF) staging post called Al Adem, where aircraft could land and refuel, and aircrew could rest before continuing onward on toward their destinations. This airstrip was exclusively for RAF aircraft. I was there when Queen Elizabeth and Prince Phillip stopped off on their way home from Kenya after they had been told the news of the death of King George.

It was a hot and arid place, and the water on the base was awful to drink. It was saline water drawn from some underwater source. It was alright for cooking and cleaning but no one wanted to drink it. It would keep us alive, but the taste was dreadful.

However, there was an old Arab man who had a small tank on the back of a cart drawn by a donkey. He was permitted to come onto our base each day to sell his water to us. It was only a couple of coins for a pint, and he would fill out chatters (an earthenware jar that kept the contents cool). It was either that or beer, and I didn't drink any alcohol. So I purchased the drinking water.

After work we would take cold showers to cool ourselves down. But we did this with our mouths and eyes kept shut. One day I noticed some men wandering around the base, and they were from an international drilling company, prospecting for oil and gas in the desert. They were a mixture of nationalities, but I think they worked for the Shell Company.

They had requested while they were in the area to use our facilities including the cinema, canteen, and showers. When they got under the running water in the shower and tasted the water, they felt sorry for us.

They spoke with our Commanding Officer asking if they might do a survey on the camp to see if they could find some better source of water for us, as a thank you. They did some work with odd instruments, running back and forth over the whole area.

One day this great drill arrived and started drilling in what was once our cricket pitch. They worked hard for about a week or ten days, and we were entertained in the evenings watching them adding the long metal rods to the ones already in the bore hole. At the end of the day they would extract the entire thing, and would remove these long rolls of rock and sand that were studied by the geologists.

Who could tell what was down there? It was all very interesting. Then one day, they said they are almost there.

Well I was working when this breakthrough took place, so I missed out on it, but what I was told was the drill head broke through the crust, and into the reservoir of water below, which came rushing up the bore hole.

It made a roaring sound like a mighty wind, then the water exploded out high into the air, drenching everyone around. The water was sweet to the taste because it was pure water. They capped it off, and put it on tap.

Sadly, the old Arab man soon stopped coming around, because we had no further need of him. The geologists presented a lecture in the air base cinema on what they had found in the drilling. It was all very interesting.

At the end they asked if there were any questions, and the one question that I was interested in was, "how come the water we used to have before you came along was so salty, but now we can drink it, because it is so sweet and refreshing?"

The geologists explained that when the Italians built the airdrome in the 1930s their excavators could not go down to the depth that modern drills could. If you only drill shallow, the water will be salty, but the deeper you drill the sweeter the water becomes, because it has to travel through solid rock that removes all the impurities, so it is pure and sweeter.

I immediately saw a message in what he had said. The deeper we go into Jesus, the sweeter his presence will be in our lives, but if we only stay in the shallows, we will not enjoy that sweet fellowship that we so desire, or the depth of faith that will see us through in times of trouble.

There is something else I remembered from that occasion, about the water rushing up like a mighty wind. It reminded me of the day of Pentecost in Acts chapter 2, when the 120 disciples were waiting for the arrival of the Holy Spirit. They heard a mighty rushing wind as the Holy Spirit descended.

The water spraying the people standing around the bore hole reminded me of the flaming tongues of fire that rested on those who were in the upper room on the day of Pentecost.

There is also a hymn that comes to mind:

Oh, the deep, deep love of Jesus,
vast unmeasured boundless free,
rolling as a mighty ocean,
in its fullness over me.

Underneath and all around me,
is the current of thy love.
Leading onward, leading homeward.
To my glorious rest above.

Oh the deep, deep love of Jesus,
Love of every love the best.
'Tis an ocean vast of blessing.
'Tis a heaven of heaven to me
and it lifts me up to Glory,
for it lifts me up to thee.

Learning to Fly

God loves the whosoever,
so that means even me.
I know He loves me
l have been told God rescued me.

He is aware of my failings,
yet he still tells me I'm important,
I am part of his eternal plan,
suddenly I'm very special,
I'm clay in the potter's hand.

He told me I'm important,
that I am a part of his family
and that there is a mansion in heaven for me
a home that is mine for eternity.
So I'm doing my best
to work toward that eternal rest.
trying to be what He wants me to be.

I've been completely restored,
I've been made whole and I am adored,
But it's nothing I have done,
yet I'm part of the family of God, it would seem.

I'm one of the chosen ones, part of His team,
I've been washed in the blood,

and given white clothes,
it's all like a glorious dream.

One day soon, I will learn to fly
because I'm going to a place
that is far away,
I can't wait to get there
to see what it's like,
with its streets of pure gold,
I may need a golden bike!

I'll be forever in glorious flight
I'm told the choir is made up of millions,
what a sound that will be
and it will be an awesome sight.

So I can't stay much longer,
my name will soon be called
I'll be receiving my wings,
and I know how to sing.

So goodbye folks I'm on my way,
I hope I shall meet you some sweet day,
in the glories of heaven.
Until that glorious day!

Picture Credits

All photographs and images in this publication are copyright © 2020 Steve Wheeler and family, except:

Cross: piqsels.com/en/public-domain-photo-jssby
Empty tomb: pixabay.com/photos/empty-tomb-nazareth-israel-3326100/
Thank NHS www.pexels.com/photo/thank-you-nhs-text-surrounded-by-hearts-4386479/
Open door: pexels.com/photo/doorway-open-door-ray-of-sunshine-stone-11380/
Thank you www.flickr.com/photos/wwworks/4759535950
Guitar: www.needpix.com/photo/download/1762424/
Sunrise: pixabay.com/photos/sunrise-sunset-nature-landscape-4404445/

Printed in Great Britain
by Amazon

44468361R00073